Beyond the Grind

Redefining Achievement Through Work-Life Integration

Introduction

In a world that glorifies hustle, many of us feel stuck in an endless cycle that steals our joy and fulfillment. Success now seems tied to exhaustion, with work and life blending into a chaotic mess of deadlines and endless tasks. You feel suffocated, like there's no end in sight. I've been there. I'm here to tell you that you don't have to sacrifice your well-being for achievement.

Work and life aren't mortal enemies but partners in a beautiful dance. This book's all about work-life balance, integration...or whatever you want to call it. A fresh way to redefine success.

As you dive in, you'll embark on a wonderful journey of self-discovery and reflection. You'll learn to set intentional goals that align with your values and prioritize self-care to fend off burnout. In a world that often equates toughness with endurance, you'll tap into a growth mindset, turning setbacks into steppingstones.

Relationships matter, too. This book will help you build a supportive framework that lifts you up. You'll see how mentorship and teamwork make the journey more enjoyable. With practical time management tips, you'll reclaim your time and make room for creativity at work. Sounds good right?

Mindfulness will be your secret weapon. You'll get to explore techniques to stay present, even when life gets a little crazy. Plus, you'll learn to use tech to enhance your life, not control it, setting boundaries for real connections.

Celebrating even the smallest of wins will shift your mindset from scarcity to abundance, reminding you of how far you've come. And failure?

You'll start seeing it as a steppingstone, not a roadblock, an essential part of growth.

Through stories and reflection, you'll find the courage to inspire others, sharing your journey to motivate those around you. As you look ahead, you'll have the tools to create a vibrant life focused on lifelong learning.

This isn't just a mere guide; it's a call to shake things up and embrace a new way of achieving. Ready to explore what it means to truly thrive?

Your fulfilling, integrated life is just around the corner!

Table of Contents

The Pomodoro Technique
and other productivity
hacks
Embracing flexibility in time
allocation

Designing spaces that
enhance creativity and
focus
The impact of
organizational culture on
performance
Encouraging a sense of
belonging and community

Practicing mindfulness to
reduce stress
Techniques for staying
present during work tasks
The benefits of meditation
for productivity

Tools and apps that support
work-life integration
Setting boundaries with
technology
The role of automation in
freeing up time

Chapter 1

The Myth of the Grind

Hold up! Let's take a moment and dig into something that's been weighing heavy on our hearts and minds—this whole hustle culture shenanigans we've found ourselves in. It's like we're all caught in this whirlwind of constant busyness, and let me tell you, it's not just exhausting; it's downright unhealthy! The idea that we got to be grinding away every single second of the day to prove our worth? Well, that's a myth, my dear friend.

Now, I get it. Society's got this annoying loudspeaker blaring about the "hustle harder" mentality. You know what I mean—those questionable motivational quotes plastered on Instagram, the endless stories of entrepreneurs working 'til dawn, and the idea that if you're not busy, you're somehow failing. It's a trap, and it's easy to fall into. But let's pause for a second and think about what that constant busyness is doing to us.

When you're always on the go, always "grinding," you're not just losing time; you're losing yourself my dear reader. The pressure to keep up can lead to burnout, anxiety, and a whole heap of other issues that nobody wants to deal with (not even your therapist!). You might feel like you're accomplishing a lot, but at what cost? Your sanity? Your relationships? Your joy? We've gotta redefine what success looks like because, let's face it, the traditional metrics just don't cut it anymore. That's the truth.

So, what does it mean to really succeed? Is it the number of hours you clock in at the office? The size of your paycheck? Or is it something deeper—like fulfillment, happiness, and a sense of balance in your life? It's high time we shift our perspective and start measuring success not by how busy we are, but by how much we're living. I don't think that we were born to 'slave' away. That's for sure!

Let's dive into this hustle culture. It's been around for ages, but it seems to have hit a fever pitch in recent years. With social media showcasing the lives of those who seem to be "doing it all," it's no wonder we feel the pressure to keep up. But here's the thing: that's not reality. What you see online is often a highlight reel, not the behind-the-scenes struggle. These fellas might not even be practicing what they preach!

Think about it—how many times have you scrolled through your IG feed, feeling like everyone else has it all figured out? It's a dangerous game. We start to equate our worth with our productivity, and before we know it, we're running on empty. We wear our busyness like a badge of honor, but it's just a recipe for disaster.

Constant busyness impacts our well-being in ways we might not even realize. It's like a slow leak in a tire—you don't notice it at first, but eventually, you're in a tough spot. Stress levels skyrocket, sleep becomes elusive, and suddenly, we're in a cycle of exhaustion that feels impossible to break. Our bodies and minds weren't built for this kind of relentless pace.

So, what do we do? We start by redefining success. Let's throw out the old playbook and write a new one, one that values balance over busyness, joy over just getting by. Success should be about how fulfilled you feel, how connected you are to your dear ones, and how much time you carve out for the things that light you up inside.

Think of success like some garden. You don't just sow seeds and walk away, right? You've gotta nurture it, give it the right amount of fertilizer and water. If you're only focused on the end result—the flowers blooming—you might forget to enjoy the process of gardening itself!

What if we started measuring success by our ability to cultivate a life that feels good? A life where we can pursue our passions without feeling like we're racing against the clock. It's about finding that sweet spot where work and life blend harmoniously, creating a rhythm that feels natural and fulfilling.

Let's be real guys: it's not about abandoning hard work. Yes, hard work has its place obviously, but it shouldn't consume your every waking moment. We need to learn how to integrate our work into our lives in a way that enhances, rather than detracts from, our well-being. It's about creating healthy boundaries, setting priorities, and understanding that it's okay to take a step back.

So, how do we get there you might ask. Baby steps my dear reader. Start by asking yourself some tough questions. What do you truly value in life? What brings you that spark of joy? What does success look like for you? Write it down. Get clear on your vision. Once you have that clarity, it's time to take action.

Consider setting boundaries around your work hours. If you're working from home, schedule a dedicated time slot to step away from your work at the end of the day. Make it a point to disconnect from emails and notifications during your downtime. Trust me, the world will keep spinning, and you'll come back refreshed and ready to tackle whatever comes your way, the next day.

And please don't forget to prioritize self-care. It's not just a trendy buzzword; it's essential. Whether it's taking a walk, reading a book, or spending time with loved ones, make time for the things that recharge your batteries. When you take care of yourself, you're better equipped to handle the demands of work and life.

Let's also talk about the power of saying "no." It's a small word, but it carries a lot of weight. If something doesn't align with your values or your vision of success, don't be afraid to decline. It's okay to prioritize your well-being over the expectations of others.

As we redefine success, let's also embrace the beauty of imperfection. Life's messy, and that's okay. You don't have to have it all figured out to be successful. In fact, some of the most inspiring stories come from those who've stumbled (even repeatedly) and learned along the way. Your journey is uniquely yours, and it's worth celebrating.

Remember hun, you're not alone in this. We're all navigating the complexities of life together. So, let's lift each other up, share our stories, and support one another as we redefine what it means to truly succeed.

In closing this chapter, let's break free from the myth of the grind. Embrace a new way of thinking—one that prioritizes well-being, balance, and fulfillment. You have the power to create a life that feels good, and it starts with redefining success on your own terms. So go ahead, take that first step. You've got this, I trust you!

Chapter 2

Embracing Work-Life Integration

Have you ever noticed how folks talk about work-life balance like it's some kind of magic trick? One minute, you're juggling deadlines, family commitments, and that ever-growing to-do list, and the next, you're trying to find that elusive "balance." But let me tell you, it's time to toss that idea out the window and embrace something much more powerful: work-life integration.

Now, what's the difference, you ask? Balance suggests that work and life are two separate entities, like oil and water. You pour one in, and it pushes the other out. It's a constant struggle, a tug-of-war that leaves you feeling drained. But integration? That's a whole different ball game. Integration means blending the two—your personal life and professional pursuits—into a harmonious symphony. It's about creating a life where work complements your personal goals, where your passions fuel your productivity, and where every aspect of your existence feeds into the other. It's a dance my dear readers, not some duel.

Imagine waking up each day, excited to tackle your work because it aligns with your values and aspirations. Picture your personal life flourishing alongside your career, rather than in spite of it. That's the beauty of work-life integration. It's about recognizing that your life is a tapestry, woven together with threads of experience, emotion, and purpose. And when you embrace this mindset, everything shifts.

So how do you blend these two worlds? Let's dive into some practical strategies that'll help you weave your personal and professional lives together seamlessly.

First off, start with intentionality. Set clear boundaries, but don't think of them as walls. Instead, think of them as flexible guidelines. Maybe you designate certain hours for deep work, but within those hours, allow yourself to take breaks that nourish your soul. A quick chat with a friend, a walk in the fresh air, or even a few minutes of meditation can recharge your batteries. The key is to be present in whatever you're doing, work or play.

Next, consider your environment. Create a workspace that inspires you. Surround yourself with items that reflect your personality and passions. Maybe it's a photo of your family, a plant that brings you joy, or a piece of art that sparks your creativity. Your space should feel like a sanctuary, not a prison.

When you love where you work, it's easier to blend those personal elements into your professional life.

Also, don't shy away from sharing your personal life with your colleagues (within reasonable measure of course). Building connections is essential. Share stories, celebrate milestones, and support each other's endeavors. When you bring your whole self to work, you create an atmosphere of authenticity and trust. It's like a warm hug on a chilly day. Everyone benefits when we foster relationships that matter.

Now, let's talk about the benefits of this holistic approach to achievement. When you integrate your work and life, you open the door to greater fulfillment. You're no longer chasing success in a vacuum; instead, you're cultivating a life that feels rich and rewarding.

Think about it my dear readers—when your personal life thrives, your professional life follows suit.

You'll find yourself more motivated, more creative, and more resilient. You'll tackle challenges with a fresh perspective because you're not weighed down by the pressure of keeping everything separate. It's like having a secret weapon in your back pocket.

Moreover, this approach fosters a sense of well-being that transcends traditional metrics of success. You'll find joy in the journey, rather than just the destination. When you're able to align your work with your passions, it's like finding a treasure chest filled with golden opportunities. You'll wake up each morning feeling inspired, ready to make a difference—not just in your life, but in the lives of others too.

A word of caution, embracing work-life integration isn't a one-time deal. It's an ongoing process. Life will throw curveballs, and that's okay. The beauty of this approach is that it allows you to adapt and evolve. You can recalibrate as needed, adjusting your strategies to fit your current reality.

So, take a moment to reflect. What does work-life integration look like for you? What steps can you take today to start blending your personal and professional lives? Maybe it's setting aside time for a hobby that fuels your passion or reaching out to a colleague to share a personal story. Whatever it is, embrace it with open arms.

As you embark on this journey, remember that you're not alone. Many folks are navigating this path, and together, we can create a community that uplifts and inspires. So, let's celebrate the beauty of integration, the joy of blending our lives, and the incredible impact it can have on our overall well-being.

You've got this. Embrace the dance of work-life integration, and watch as your life transforms into a beautiful, harmonious masterpiece. The world is waiting for your unique contributions, and when you integrate your passions with your profession, there's no limit to what you can achieve. Now, go on and take that first step—you're closer than you think!

Chapter 3

Setting Intentional Goals

When it comes to setting goals, let's get one thing straight: it ain't just about writing down a list and hoping for the best. Nah, my friend, it's about crafting meaningful and achievable objectives that light a fire in your belly. You want goals that make you leap outta bed in the morning, ready to tackle the day. So, let's roll up our sleeves and dive into the art of intentional goal-setting, shall we?

First off, think about what truly matters to you. What gets you pumped? What stirs your soul? These are the questions that'll help you craft those meaningful objectives. You see, when your goals align with your personal values, they become more than just tasks on a to-do list; they morph into steppingstones on your path to fulfillment. Picture this: you're not just chasing a promotion at work because it looks good on paper. You're pursuing it because it aligns with your value of growth and contribution. That's where the magic happens!

Now, let's talk about making those objectives achievable. Setting the bar too high can feel like trying to leap over a mountain. Instead, break it down into smaller, bite-sized pieces. It's like building a house—start with a solid foundation. Set specific, measurable, attainable, relevant, and time-bound (SMART) goals. This framework isn't just a fancy acronym; it's a roadmap to success. For example, instead of saying, "I wanna be healthier," try, "I'll walk for 30 minutes every day for the next month." See how much clearer that is? You're not just dreaming; you're doing!

And here's the thing—flexibility is key in this whole goal-setting game. Life's unpredictable, and sometimes the best-laid plans go awry. But that doesn't mean you throw in the towel! Think of your goals like a river—sometimes it flows smoothly, and other times it hits a rock and has to change course. Embrace that flexibility. If something isn't working, don't be afraid to pivot. Maybe you planned to hit the gym five times a week, but life got busy. Instead, aim for three solid workouts and sprinkle in some home exercises. Adapt, adjust, and keep moving forward.

Let's dig a little deeper into aligning your personal values with your professional aspirations. It's like two sides of the same coin, and when they match up, you'll find a sense of purpose that drives you. Take a moment to jot down your core values. What do you stand for? Is it integrity, creativity, or community? Once you've got that list, look at your professional goals and see how they fit together. If you value creativity, but your job feels like a dull routine, it's time to shake things up. Maybe you can propose a new project that allows you to express that creativity.

Aligning your goals with your values creates a sense of harmony in your life. It's like playing your favorite song on repeat—it just feels right!

Now, let's not forget the importance of being flexible with your goals. Life is like a dance, my friend; sometimes you gotta change your steps. If you find yourself hitting a wall or feeling stuck, don't panic! It's a chance to reassess. Maybe your original goal needs a little tweaking, or perhaps you've discovered a new passion along the way. That's all part of the journey! Remember, flexibility doesn't mean giving up; it means being open to new possibilities.

To put it all together, let's create a simple action plan. Grab a piece of paper or open up a fresh document on your computer. Write down one or two meaningful goals that resonate with your values. Make sure they're achievable and break them down into smaller steps. Then, add a note to remind yourself to stay flexible. Life's a wild ride and being adaptable will help you navigate those twists and turns.

As you embark on this journey of setting intentional goals, keep in mind that you're not alone. Every small step you take is a step toward a more fulfilling life. Celebrate those wins, no matter how tiny they may seem. You're building a future that reflects who you truly are, and that's something to be proud of.

So, let's lace up those boots and get moving! You've got this, and the world is waiting for you to shine. Remember, it's not just about reaching the destination; it's about enjoying the ride along the way. With each goal you set, you're not just chasing success; you're creating a life that feels authentic and vibrant. Embrace the journey, and let's make those dreams a reality!

Chapter 4

Prioritizing Self-Care

We live in a world that often glorifies the grind, don't we? But let me tell you, if you don't take care of yourself, that grind can turn into a slippery slope straight to burnout. Recognizing the signs of burnout is the first step in turning things around. You might feel more tired than usual, even after a good night's sleep. Or maybe you're irritable, snapping at folks for no reason. If you find yourself dragging through the day, struggling to focus, or feeling like you're just going through the motions, it's time to hit the brakes and take a good, hard look at what's going on.

Burnout isn't just a fancy term for being tired. It's a state of emotional, physical, and mental exhaustion caused by prolonged and excessive stress. Think of it like a car running on empty; eventually, it won't go anywhere. You've got to refuel. So, how do you do that? By prioritizing self-care in your daily routine.

Now, I know what you might be thinking: "I don't have time for self-care!" But hear me out. Self-care doesn't have to be a whole day at the spa or a week-long vacation in the Bahamas. It can be as simple as taking five minutes to breathe deeply, stepping outside for a quick walk, or even indulging in a favorite hobby. You've got to find those little pockets of time in your day to check in with yourself.

Incorporating self-care practices into your daily routine is like adding a secret ingredient to your favorite recipe. It doesn't take much, but it makes all the difference. Start small. Maybe you set a timer for five minutes to practice mindfulness or meditation. Or you take a break to stretch your legs every hour.

How about setting aside time each week for something you love—reading, painting, or even just watching your favorite show? The key is consistency. Make it a non-negotiable part of your day.

And let's not forget about the role of mental health in sustainable success. When you're feeling good mentally, everything else falls into place. You become more productive, more creative, and more resilient. It's like a ripple effect. When you take care of your mental health, you're not just doing yourself a favor; you're setting yourself up for long-term success.

Here's a little exercise for you. Grab a piece of paper and jot down three self-care practices you can easily incorporate into your daily life. Maybe it's a morning routine that includes a few minutes of journaling, or perhaps it's a nightly wind-down ritual with a cup of tea and a good book. Whatever it is, write it down and commit to it. You'll be amazed at how these small changes can lead to a big impact on your overall well-being.

Now, let's talk about boundaries. It's essential to set boundaries around your time and energy. This means saying no when you need to, stepping back from obligations that drain you, and prioritizing activities that lift you up. Remember, you can't pour from an empty cup. Fill your cup first, and then you'll have plenty to give to others.

As you embark on this journey of prioritizing self-care, keep in mind that it's not a one-and-done deal. It's an ongoing process. You'll have good days and bad days, and that's perfectly okay. The important thing is to be gentle with yourself. If you slip up and find yourself back in the grind, don't beat yourself up. Just recognize it, adjust, and keep moving forward.

You've got the power to redefine what success looks like for you. It doesn't have to be all about the hustle and bustle. It can be about finding joy in the little things, creating a life that feels good, and embracing the beautiful mess that is life.

So, here's to you and your journey. Celebrate the small wins along the way, whether that's taking a moment for yourself or recognizing when you need to take a step back. You're not just a cog in the machine; you're a vibrant, valuable human being. And you deserve to thrive, not just survive.

Incorporate self-care into your daily routine, recognize the signs of burnout, and remember that your mental health is the foundation of your success. It's all connected, and you have the power to create a life that feels balanced and fulfilling. You can do this! Embrace the journey, and let's redefine achievement together.

Chapter 5

Cultivating a Growth Mindset

You know, life ain't always a straight road. Sometimes it's more like a winding path through a cornfield—full of twists, turns, and unexpected bumps. But here's the thing, the secret to navigating that path lies in cultivating a growth mindset. It's about embracing resilience, learning from our missteps, and fostering a culture of continuous learning. Let's dig into this together, shall we?

First off, let's talk about resilience and adaptability. Life's gonna throw curveballs, no doubt about it. But how do we respond to those challenges? That's what really counts. Resilience is like that sturdy oak tree that bends in the wind but doesn't break. You've got to learn to bend, my friend. Adaptability is your trusty sidekick on this journey. When plans go awry—and they will—being adaptable means you can pivot, adjust, and keep moving forward. It's like dancing in the rain instead of waiting for the storm to pass.

Now, let's not sugarcoat it—failure is part of the game. It's like a badge of honor for those of us striving for something more. But remember, every setback is a setup for a comeback. Think of failure as your greatest teacher. It's where the real lessons lie, waiting for you to discover them. When you stumble, take a moment to reflect. What went wrong? What can you learn from it? Remember, the most successful people out there didn't get to where they are without facing a few bumps along the way. They embraced those bumps, learned from them, and kept on truckin'.

And while we're at it, let's chat about fostering a culture of continuous learning. This ain't just about hitting the books; it's about having a curious mind and a heart that's open to new experiences. It's like being a kid again, always asking "why" and "how." Surround yourself with people who inspire you to learn, grow, and think differently. Create an environment where questions are encouraged, and exploration is celebrated.

Now, I want you to picture this: you're in a room full of folks, all eager to share their experiences and insights. It's electric! That's the power of a learning culture. It sparks creativity and innovation. When you're part of a community that values growth, you'll find yourself stepping outside your comfort zone, trying new things, and pushing the boundaries of what you thought was possible.

So, how do you put this all into practice? Let's break it down into some actionable steps.

1. **Embrace challenges**. Instead of shying away from tough situations, lean into them. Ask yourself, "What can I learn from this?"

2. **Reflect on your failures**. Keep a journal, jot down your thoughts after a setback. What did you learn? How can you apply that moving forward?

3. **Surround yourself with growth-minded people**. Find a mentor or join a group that encourages learning and exploration.

4. **Set aside time for continuous learning**. Whether it's reading a book, taking an online course, or attending a workshop, make it a priority.

5. **Celebrate small wins**. Recognize your progress, no matter how small. It'll keep you motivated and reinforce that growth mindset.

Now, let's not forget the importance of patience in this process. Growth takes time. It's like planting a seed and nurturing it until it blooms. You may not see immediate results, but trust that your efforts are laying the groundwork for something beautiful.

Picture yourself a year from now, looking back at how far you've come. Each challenge you faced, each lesson you learned—it's all part of your story. You're not just surviving; you're thriving. You're a testament to what it means to cultivate a growth mindset.

And remember, it's okay to stumble along the way. What matters is that you get back up, dust yourself off, and keep moving forward. You've got this! Embrace the journey and let your growth mindset lead the way. The world is waiting for your brilliance to shine through.

As we wrap up this chapter, take a moment to reflect on your own journey. What challenges have you faced? What lessons have you learned? Write them down. Acknowledge your resilience and adaptability. And let that spark a fire within you to keep pushing forward, learning, and growing.

You're not just redefining achievement; you're redefining what it means to live a fulfilling life. So, let's keep this momentum going. The best is yet to come!

Chapter 6

Building Supportive Relationships

You know, when it comes to crafting a life that feels fulfilling and rich, there's one golden thread that weaves it all together: relationships. Not just any relationships, mind you, but the kind that lift you up, inspire you, and push you to be the best version of yourself. Let's dive into the heart of this, shall we?

Networking and collaboration ain't just buzzwords; they're the lifeblood of progress. Picture this: you're at a crossroads in your career, feeling a bit stuck. You've got the drive, but maybe you're missing that spark of inspiration. Now, imagine you attend a local meetup or a workshop. You start chatting with folks, sharing ideas, and suddenly, you're buzzing with new energy. That's the power of connection! Networking isn't just about swapping business cards; it's about building a community of like-minded souls who can uplift each other.

Think of it like planting a garden. You don't just throw seeds in the ground and hope for the best. You nurture those seeds, water them, and give them sunlight. The same goes for your relationships. You've got to invest time and energy into them. Reach out to someone you admire. Ask them for coffee. Share your dreams and challenges. You'd be surprised how much you can learn from others' experiences. It's a two-way street, and the more you give, the more you'll receive.

Now, let's talk about the magic of nurturing relationships that inspire and uplift. This isn't about surrounding yourself with people who simply agree with you. No, my friend, it's about finding those who challenge you, who make you think deeper and push you out of your comfort zone. It's like having a personal cheerleading squad, but one that's not afraid to give you a reality check when you need it.

Think about your circle for a moment. Who's in it? Are they the kind of folks who lift you up, or do they drain your energy? Surrounding yourself with positive, supportive people is crucial. These are the ones who will celebrate your wins, no matter how small, and stand by you during the tough times. They'll remind you of your worth when you forget.

Mentorship plays a pivotal role in this whole equation. Having a mentor is like having a lighthouse guiding you through the fog. They've been where you are and can offer insights that come from experience. Whether it's a formal arrangement or a casual friendship, a mentor can provide perspective that you might not see on your own.

But here's the truth, mentorship isn't just a one-way street. You've got to be open to learning, and that means being vulnerable. Share your struggles, ask questions, and be willing to take their advice to heart. And don't forget, you can be a mentor too! You don't have to be a seasoned pro to guide someone else. Your unique experiences and insights can be invaluable to someone just starting out.

Let's break it down into some actionable steps, shall we?

1. **Expand Your Network**: Attend events, workshops, or even online webinars. Don't be shy! Strike up conversations and make genuine connections.

2. **Nurture Your Relationships**: Check in on friends and colleagues. Send a quick text or an email just to say you're thinking of them. It doesn't have to

be elaborate; just a simple "Hey, how's it going?" can mean the world.

3. **Seek Out Mentorship**: Identify someone you admire in your field. Reach out and ask if they'd be willing to chat. Prepare some questions in advance to make the most of your time together.

4. **Be a Mentor**: Look for opportunities to help others. Whether it's through formal programs or informal friendships, share your knowledge and experiences.

5. **Create a Supportive Environment**: Surround yourself with people who inspire you. This might mean reevaluating some relationships and making room for those who truly uplift you.

As you embark on this journey of building supportive relationships, remember it's not just about what you can get; it's about what you can give. Each connection you make is a chance to create something beautiful, something that enriches not just your life but the lives of others.

So, take a moment to visualize the relationships you want to cultivate. Picture yourself surrounded by people who inspire you, who challenge you, and who cheer you on. Feel that energy? That's the magic of connection. You've got this!

Now, go out there and start building those relationships. You never know how one conversation, one connection, or one moment of vulnerability can change the course of your life. Let's get to it!

Chapter 7

Time Management Reimagined

You know, time management ain't just about cramming more into your day. It's about rethinking how you approach the hours you've got. It's like cooking a stew; you gotta know when to add the ingredients for the best flavor. Let's dive into some techniques that'll help you prioritize effectively, explore nifty productivity hacks like the Pomodoro Technique, and embrace a little flexibility in how you allocate your time.

First up, prioritization. It's the bread and butter of time management. So, picture this: you wake up in the morning, and your to-do list looks like a novel—long, daunting, and a bit overwhelming. What do you do? You gotta sift through that list and figure out what's truly important. Start by identifying your big rocks—the tasks that'll move the needle for you.

One effective technique is the **Eisenhower Matrix**. It's a simple tool that helps you categorize tasks into four quadrants: urgent and important, important but not urgent, urgent but not important, and neither urgent nor important. When sorting your tasks this way, you'll quickly see what needs your attention right now and what can wait.

Next, let's chat about the **Pomodoro Technique**. This nifty little method is my secret weapon for productivity. Here's how it works: you set a timer for 25 minutes and focus on a single task until the timer goes off. Once that bell dings, take a 5-minute break. It's like a mini vacation for your brain. After four rounds, treat yourself to a longer break—15 to 30 minutes. This technique keeps your mind fresh and helps prevent burnout. You'd be surprised how much you can accomplish in those focused bursts.

But hold on a second. Life's not always about rigid schedules and ticking boxes. Sometimes, you gotta roll with the punches. Embracing flexibility in your time allocation is key. Think of it like dancing. You gotta know the steps, but sometimes you just gotta sway to the music. When unexpected things pop up, like a surprise meeting or a family emergency, be ready to adjust your plans.

Here's a practical tip: at the start of each week, take a few moments to review your priorities. Look at what's coming up and adjust your time blocks accordingly. If you see a big project looming, maybe you need to shuffle some tasks around to make room for it. That way, you're not just reacting to life; you're proactively managing your time in a way that feels right for you.

Now, let's talk about the art of saying no. This is a biggie, folks. It's tempting to say yes to every request that comes your way, but that can lead to overwhelm faster than a runaway train. Remember, every time you say yes to something, you're saying no to something else. So, be mindful of your commitments. If a task doesn't align with your goals or values, don't hesitate to decline. Your time is precious, and you deserve to spend it on what truly matters to you.

As you embrace these techniques, keep in mind that time management is a journey, not a destination. You're not gonna nail it overnight. It's about finding what works for you and tweaking it along the way. Celebrate those small wins! Finished a project ahead of schedule? Treat yourself! Mastered the Pomodoro Technique? Give yourself a high-five! Each step forward is a step toward a more integrated life.

To wrap it all up, effective time management is about prioritizing what matters, using tools like the Pomodoro Technique to enhance productivity, and remaining flexible to adapt to life's surprises. It's a dance, a balance, and above all, a journey of growth. One step at a time my lovely readers.

Chapter 8

Creating a Purpose-Driven Work Environment

Designing a workspace is like painting a canvas—each brushstroke contributes to the final masterpiece. When you think about creating a purpose-driven work environment, envision spaces that not only look good but also spark creativity and enhance focus. You want your team to feel inspired when they walk in, right? A vibrant environment can be a game-changer. Consider adding elements like natural light, plants, and comfortable seating. You might even throw in some funky art or a community board where folks can share ideas. These little touches create an atmosphere that encourages innovation and keeps minds sharp.

But hold on a second! It's not just about aesthetics. The heart of your organization lies in its culture. Think of culture as the soil in which your team grows. If the soil is rich and nurturing, your team will thrive. A positive organizational culture boosts performance and keeps morale high. When people feel valued and respected, they're more likely to go the extra mile. They'll collaborate, share ideas, and push each other to be better. That's the magic of a supportive culture—it transforms individuals into a cohesive unit.

Now, let's talk about belonging. Everybody wants to feel like they fit in, right? When you foster a sense of community, you create a workplace where everyone feels included. This isn't just about social gatherings; it's about cultivating genuine connections. Encourage team-building activities that allow folks to bond over shared interests.

Celebrate achievements, big or small, and create rituals that strengthen camaraderie. When your team feels a sense of belonging, they're more engaged and committed. It's like adding fuel to a fire; their passion for the work will ignite and spread throughout the organization.

So, how do you weave these elements together? Start by assessing your current environment. Walk through your space with fresh eyes. Is it inspiring? Does it encourage collaboration? If not, it's time to make some changes. Gather feedback from your team. Ask them what they need to feel more creative and engaged. Their insights will guide you in designing spaces that truly resonate with them.

Next, invest in training that emphasizes the importance of culture. Host workshops that focus on teamwork, communication, and respect. Encourage leaders to model the behavior you want to see. When leaders embody the values of the organization, it sets the tone for everyone else. Remember, culture is not just a policy; it's a daily practice.

Now, let's sprinkle in some practical tips. Create designated areas for collaboration, quiet work, and relaxation. This way, your team can choose the environment that best suits their needs at any given moment. A cozy nook with soft lighting can be perfect for brainstorming, while a bright, open space can energize a team meeting. The key is to offer variety—people thrive in different settings.

Don't forget about the power of recognition. Regularly acknowledge hard work and celebrate milestones. It doesn't have to be grand; even a simple shout-out in a team meeting can make someone's day. When people feel appreciated, they're more likely to contribute their best efforts.

As you build this purpose-driven work environment, keep in mind that it's a journey, not a destination. Stay open to feedback and be willing to adapt. The needs of your team may change over time, and that's okay. Embrace the evolution of your culture and workspace as a sign of growth.

In the end, creating a purpose-driven work environment is about more than just productivity. It's about nurturing creativity, fostering connections, and building a community where everyone can thrive. When you design spaces that inspire and cultivate a culture of belonging, you're not just enhancing performance—you're transforming lives. And that, my friend, is the true essence of achievement.

So, take a deep breath, roll up those sleeves, and get to work. Your team is counting on you to create a space where they can flourish. Together, you'll redefine what it means to succeed. Now, go out there and make it happen!

Chapter 9

Mindfulness in the Workplace

In the whirlwind of deadlines and to-do lists, it's easy to lose sight of what truly matters. Stress creeps in like an uninvited guest, and before you know it, your mind's racing a mile a minute. But here's the thing—practicing mindfulness can be your secret weapon against that relentless pressure. It's not just about sitting cross-legged and chanting "om." No, it's about being present, about tuning in to the moment, and letting the chaos of the day fade into the background.

So, you're at your desk, the phone's ringing, emails are piling up, and your brain feels like a crowded highway. Instead of getting swept away in that current, take a step back. Close your eyes for a moment—yes, I mean it! Just breathe. Inhale deeply through your nose, hold it for a beat, and then exhale slowly. Feel that? That's the sweet relief of mindfulness washing over you. It's like a refreshing breeze on a hot summer day, clearing away the cobwebs and letting clarity shine through.

Now, let's talk about techniques for staying present during work tasks. You've got your coffee, your playlist, and maybe even a little plant on your desk. But what about your mind? It's time to bring it back to the here and now. One effective way to do this is through the practice of single tasking. That's right—put aside that multitasking myth. Focus on one task at a time. Give it your full attention, as if it were the most important thing in the world. Because, at that moment, it is.

You can also set mini mindfulness breaks throughout your day. Maybe it's a quick stretch, a brief walk, or even a few minutes of just staring out the window. Use these moments to reset your mind. When you come back to your work, you'll be amazed at how much sharper your focus is. It's like wiping the fog off your glasses and seeing the world clearly again.

And let's not forget about the magic of meditation. You might think, "I don't have time for that!" But hear me out—just a few minutes of meditation can transform your productivity. Studies show that regular meditation can boost your attention span and improve your ability to concentrate. It's like giving your brain a workout, strengthening those mental muscles so you can tackle your tasks with renewed vigor.

So, how do you get started? Find a quiet spot, sit comfortably, and focus on your breath. Let thoughts drift in and out like clouds in the sky. If your mind wanders, gently guide it back to your breath. Start with just five minutes a day. You'll be surprised at how quickly those minutes add up and how much more centered you feel.

Now, let's dive deeper into the benefits of meditation for productivity. When you meditate, you're not just sitting in silence; you're training your mind to be more resilient. You're building a fortress against stress, anxiety, and distractions. This newfound clarity translates directly to your work. You'll find that you can tackle complex projects with greater ease, make decisions more confidently, and engage with your colleagues more effectively.

And let's not overlook the emotional benefits. Mindfulness fosters a sense of calm that ripples through your day. When you're grounded and centered, you're less likely to react impulsively to challenges. Instead of snapping at a coworker or feeling overwhelmed by a deadline, you'll respond with grace and poise. You'll be the calm in the storm, and trust me, people will notice.

But remember, it's a journey, not a race. Start small. Incorporate these mindfulness practices into your daily routine and celebrate the progress you make along the way. Maybe you'll notice you're less stressed, or perhaps you'll find joy in the little things. Each step forward is a victory, and every moment of mindfulness is a chance to connect with yourself and your work on a deeper level.

As you embrace mindfulness in the workplace, visualize the impact it will have on your life. Imagine walking into your office feeling calm and focused, ready to take on whatever comes your way. Picture yourself navigating challenges with a sense of ease, your mind clear and your heart open. This is the power of mindfulness—it's not just about surviving the grind; it's about thriving in it.

So, let's wrap this up with a little pep talk. You've got this! You have the tools and the wisdom to create a more mindful work environment. Embrace these practices, and watch as your productivity soars and your stress melts away. You're not just redefining achievement; you're redefining what it means to work with purpose and joy.

Take a deep breath, my friend. The journey of mindfulness is yours to explore. Each moment is a gift, and with every mindful choice, you're crafting a life that's not just about work, but about fulfillment, balance, and joy. Now, go out there and shine!

Chapter 10

Leveraging Technology for Balance

In this fast-paced world, technology can feel like a double-edged sword. It's a friend and a foe all wrapped up in one shiny device. But here's the thing: when you learn to leverage it wisely, it can be your best ally in achieving that sweet work-life integration we all crave. Let's dig into the tools and strategies that'll help you make technology work for you, not against you.

First up, let's talk about the treasure trove of tools and apps out there. There's a plethora of options that can support your work-life integration journey. Think of them as your trusty sidekicks. You've got task management apps like Trello or Asana that help you keep track of your projects and deadlines. They let you visualize your tasks, break 'em down, and prioritize like a pro. Then there's calendar apps—Google Calendar is a classic—where you can block out time for work, family, and self-care. It's all about creating that roadmap for your day.

And don't forget about communication tools! Slack, Mattermost or Microsoft Teams can streamline your work chats, keeping everything organized and reducing the noise. You can even set up channels for specific projects or interests. This way, you're not just juggling a million conversations but focusing on what truly matters.

Please keep in mind that technology is only as good as the boundaries you set around it. You gotta be the boss of your tech, not the other way around. So, how do you do that? Start by establishing some clear boundaries. When you clock out for the day, put your phone on 'do not disturb'. You wouldn't want your work emails buzzing in while you're trying to enjoy a family dinner or some much needed "me time."

Another powerful strategy is to create tech-free zones in your home. Maybe it's the dining room or the bedroom—places where you can disconnect from screens and reconnect with the people and things that fill your heart. Trust me, it's a game changer. You'll find that the world doesn't fall apart if you step away from your devices for a bit. In fact, you might just find more clarity and peace.

Now, let's chat about automation. This is where the magic really happens. Automation can be your secret weapon for freeing up time. Think about the repetitive tasks that eat away at your day. Whether it's sending out emails, scheduling social media posts, or managing invoices, there's likely a tool out there that can handle it for you.

Take Zapier, for instance. It connects different apps and automates workflows, saving you precious minutes. Imagine having your email newsletters automatically sent out or your social media posts scheduled weeks in advance. That's time you can reclaim for more meaningful activities, like pursuing a hobby or spending quality time with loved ones.

And here's a little tip: start small with automation. Choose one or two tasks that take up too much of your time and find a way to automate them. You'll be amazed at how quickly you can free up your schedule. It's like giving yourself a gift of time.

As you embrace these tools and strategies, remember that technology is a means to an end. It's there to enhance your life, not complicate it. So, take a moment to reflect on what truly matters to you. What are your priorities? What brings you joy? Use technology to support those priorities, not distract from them.

In the end, it's all about finding that sweet spot where technology serves you. It's about creating a life that feels balanced and fulfilling. When you harness the power of these tools, set those boundaries, and embrace automation, you're not just surviving the grind—you're thriving in it.

So, take a deep breath, my friend. You've got this. Embrace the tech, set your boundaries, and watch as you carve out a life that feels whole and integrated. Your journey towards work-life integration is just beginning, and the possibilities are endless.

Chapter 11

Celebrating Small Wins

You know, it's easy to get lost in the hustle, chasing after the big milestones, the shiny trophies that symbolize success. The truth is that it's the small wins that truly pave the way to those grand achievements. Recognizing progress in your journey is like planting seeds in a garden. You water them, nurture them, and before you know it, you've got a beautiful bloom to show for your efforts!

Let's take a moment to appreciate that. Every little step you take, every task you complete, is a victory worth celebrating. Did you finish that report on time? Win! Did you manage to take a lunch break instead of working through it? Double win! These small victories create momentum, and momentum is the wind beneath your wings. It's what propels you forward, giving you the energy to tackle the next challenge.

Now, let's dive into the psychological benefits of celebrating these achievements. When you acknowledge your successes, no matter how small, you're sending a message to your brain that says, "Hey, I'm doing something right!" This boosts your self-esteem and cultivates a positive mindset. It's like a little pat on the back, a reminder that you're capable and moving in the right direction.

Research shows that celebrating achievements releases dopamine, that feel-good hormone that elevates your mood and enhances your motivation. Think of it as your brain's way of rewarding you for your hard work. So, when you recognize your progress, you're not just boosting your spirits; you're building a psychological foundation for future success.

But how do you make this celebration a part of your routine? Well, let's talk about creating rituals for acknowledging successes. Rituals are powerful. They give structure to our lives and help us mark significant moments. Maybe it's treating yourself to a favorite snack after completing a project or taking a moment to reflect and jot down your achievements in a journal.

Here's a fun idea: why not create a "Win Jar"? Every time you achieve something—big or small—write it down on a slip of paper and toss it in the jar. When you're feeling low or doubting your progress, pull out a few slips and remind yourself of all the great things you've accomplished. It's a tangible reminder that you're on the right path, even when the journey gets tough.

Another ritual could be sharing your wins with a friend or family member. This not only reinforces your achievement but also invites others to celebrate with you. It's like throwing a mini party for yourself— who doesn't love a little confetti in their life?

As you cultivate these rituals, remember that they don't have to be elaborate. Simplicity is key. Whether it's a moment of gratitude, a small treat, or a quick text to a friend, find what resonates with you. The goal is to make celebration a habit, something that becomes second nature as you navigate through your days.

So, let's wrap this up with a little pep talk. Life's journey is filled with ups and downs, twists and turns. But in the midst of it all, don't forget to pause and celebrate those small wins. They're the steppingstones to your greater achievements.

They're the little joys that make the grind worthwhile.

You've got this! Embrace your progress, celebrate your victories, and create those rituals that remind you just how far you've come. The path to success isn't just about the destination; it's about savoring every moment along the way. So go ahead, pop that confetti, and let the world know that you're making strides—one small win at a time.

Chapter 12

Redefining Failure

Failure. Just the word alone can send shivers down the spine, can't it? It's a four-letter word that looms over us like a storm cloud, threatening to rain on our parade. But what if I told you that failure isn't the end of the road? What if it's more like a detour sign, guiding you toward a new path, a new opportunity? That's the heart of this chapter, folks. It's about flipping the script on failure and seeing it as a steppingstone to success.

Let me share a little story with you. A few years back, I tried my hand at launching a small business. I had big dreams and even bigger plans. I poured my heart and soul into it, and then— boom! —it crashed and burned. I felt like I'd been hit by a freight train. But after I dusted myself off and picked up the pieces, I realized something profound: every mistake, every misstep, taught me valuable lessons. I learned about resilience, about creativity, and about the importance of being adaptable. That experience, painful as it was, became a crucial part of my journey. It shaped me into the person I am today.

You see, failure is not a dirty word; it's an essential part of the growth process. Think about it like this: when you learn to walk, you stumble. You fall. But you get back up, don't you? You keep trying until you find your balance. That's the spirit of experimentation and innovation. When you embrace failure, you open yourself up to new ideas and fresh perspectives. You create a culture where it's okay to take risks and think outside the box.

Imagine a workplace where everyone feels safe to share their wild ideas, no matter how outlandish they may seem. A place where people are encouraged to experiment, to try things that might not work out. This kind of environment fosters creativity and collaboration. It's like a garden, where diverse ideas can grow and flourish. And guess what? Some of those ideas will blossom into something beautiful, something transformative.

Now, let's talk about how to cultivate this culture of experimentation. Start by encouraging open dialogue. Create spaces where team members can share their thoughts without fear of judgment. Celebrate the attempts, not just the successes. When someone takes a leap and it doesn't pan out, recognize their courage. That's how you build a supportive community, one where everyone feels valued and empowered to take risks.

And don't forget the power of storytelling. Share your own experiences of failure. When you're vulnerable and open about your challenges, it creates a bond with others. It shows them they're not alone in their struggles. It's like a warm hug on a cold day—comforting and reassuring. You're paving the way for others to feel safe in their own journeys.

Let's get practical for a moment. Here are a few steps you can take to redefine failure in your life and work:

1. **Reframe your mindset**: Instead of seeing failure as a setback, view it as an opportunity to learn and grow. Ask yourself, "What can I take away from this experience?" Shift your focus from the negative to the potential for improvement.

2. **Share your stories**: Be open about your failures with others. Your vulnerability can inspire those around you to embrace their own challenges. Create a culture of storytelling, where everyone feels encouraged to share their journeys.

3. **Experiment regularly**: Make it a habit to try new things, whether in your personal life or at work. Encourage your team to brainstorm and test out ideas, no matter how unconventional they may seem. Celebrate the effort, even if the outcome isn't what you expected.

4. **Foster a supportive environment**: Build a culture where people feel safe to take risks. Recognize and reward those who step outside their comfort zones. Let them know that their efforts are valued, regardless of the results.

5. **Reflect and learn**: After a setback, take the time to reflect on what happened. What went well? What didn't? Use these insights to inform your next steps and to refine your approach.

As we wrap up this chapter, remember this: failure is not the enemy. It's a teacher, a guide, and a steppingstone on your journey to success. Embrace it, learn from it, and let it propel you forward. You've got this! Your path is uniquely yours, and every stumble along the way is just part of the dance. So go ahead—step boldly into the unknown and redefine what it means to fail. The world is waiting for your brilliance!

Chapter 13

The Power of Reflection

Life moves fast, doesn't it? One minute you're chasing dreams, and the next, you're wondering if you've even stopped to catch your breath. That's where the power of reflection comes in. It's like hitting the pause button on your favorite song, allowing the melody to settle in your heart before you dance to the next beat. Reflection isn't just a nice-to-have; it's essential for growth and clarity. So, let's dig into how you can harness this powerful tool to fuel your journey toward work-life integration.

First off, self-assessment is your best buddy when it comes to understanding where you stand. Think of it like checking the oil in your car. You wouldn't want to drive cross-country without knowing if you're running on fumes, right? Regular self-assessment gives you the chance to evaluate your progress, strengths, and areas that might need a little extra TLC.

Now my beloved readers, how do you go about it? Simple techniques can help. Start with a SWOT analysis—yeah, I know it sounds fancy but stick with me. You identify your Strengths, Weaknesses, Opportunities, and Threats. Grab a piece of paper and draw four boxes. In the first box, jot down what you're good at—your strengths. In the second, list what you need to work on—your weaknesses. The third box is for opportunities, those golden chances that could help you grow. Finally, in the last box, write down any threats that might be holding you back. This little exercise can provide you with a roadmap for personal growth, and it's a great way to keep your goals aligned with your values.

Now, let's talk about journaling. Oh boy, journaling! It's like having a heart-to-heart with yourself. When you put pen to paper, you're not just writing; you're unlocking doors to clarity and insight. There's something magical about seeing your thoughts laid out in front of you. It's like shining a flashlight into the dark corners of your mind. You might be surprised at what you find.

Start by setting aside a few minutes each day. Find a cozy spot, grab your favorite notebook, and let the words flow. Don't worry about grammar or spelling—this isn't a term paper. Write freely about your day, your feelings, and your dreams. You can even use prompts if you're feeling stuck. "What made me smile today?" or "What's one thing I learned about myself this week?" can spark a wealth of insights. The key is to be honest and open with yourself. Journaling is a safe space for exploration, and it can help you connect the dots in your life.

Please bear in mind that reflection isn't a one-and-done deal. It's important to check in with yourself regularly. Think of it like tuning a guitar. If you don't tune it often, the music won't sound quite right. Set aside time each week—maybe Sunday mornings with a cup of coffee—to reflect on your past week. Ask yourself what went well, what didn't, and what you want to change moving forward. It's a chance to celebrate your small wins and learn from your missteps.

And let's not forget the power of gratitude in this process. When you reflect, take a moment to jot down what you're grateful for. It shifts your mindset from what's lacking to what's abundant in your life. Gratitude is like sunshine for your soul—it helps you bloom, even on the toughest days.

So, how do these practices tie into work-life integration? Well, when you take the time to reflect, you're giving yourself the gift of clarity. You're better equipped to align your personal and professional goals. You'll start to see patterns in your behavior and thoughts that might be hindering your progress. And trust me, that's where the magic happens.

Imagine sitting down at the end of a long week, flipping through your journal, and seeing how far you've come. You might notice that you've been spending too much time on tasks that don't light you up or that you're neglecting your personal passions. Reflection helps you recalibrate, ensuring that you're living a life that feels fulfilling and authentic.

Now, let's get practical. Here's a quick checklist to help you implement these techniques:

1. **Set aside dedicated time** for self-assessment—weekly, monthly, or quarterly. Find what works best for you.

2. **Try a SWOT analysis** to identify your strengths, weaknesses, opportunities, and threats.

3. **Commit to journaling daily or weekly**. Choose a time that feels right—morning, night, or whenever you can carve out a few moments.

4. **Reflect on your week regularly**. Celebrate your wins, learn from your setbacks, and adjust your goals as needed.

5. **Incorporate gratitude into your reflection practice.** Write down at least three things you're grateful for each week.

Remember, this journey is yours, and it's meant to be a joyful one. Reflection isn't just about looking back; it's about forging ahead with newfound insight and purpose. It's the compass that guides you through the winding roads of life, helping you navigate the twists and turns with confidence.

As you embrace the power of reflection, visualize the impact it will have on your life. Picture yourself feeling more grounded, more aware, and more in tune with your goals. Imagine the sense of clarity washing over you as you align your actions with your values. This is not just about achieving more; it's about living more fully.

You've got this! Keep that journal close, and don't shy away from those check-ins. They're your secret weapon in the quest for work-life integration. As you reflect, remember that every thought, every feeling, and every insight is a steppingstone toward the life you desire. So go ahead—embrace the power of reflection, and watch as your journey unfolds in ways you never thought possible.

Chapter 14

Inspiring Others Through Your Journey

When you step into the light and share your story, you ignite a spark in others. It's like tossing a pebble into a still pond—the ripples spread out, touching lives you might never even know about. Your journey, with all its ups and downs, has the power to uplift and motivate. It's a gift that keeps on giving.

Think about it. Every challenge you've faced, every lesson you've learned, has shaped you into who you are today. And that's a story worth telling. When you share your experiences, you're not just talking about yourself; you're creating a connection. You're saying, "Hey, I've been there too. If I can do it, so can you." It's a simple yet profound message that resonates deeply.

Imagine sitting around a campfire with friends, sharing tales of your struggles and triumphs. That warmth, that camaraderie—it's contagious. When you open up, you invite others to do the same. Suddenly, you're not just a lone traveler on this journey; you're part of a community. A community built on shared experiences, empathy, and understanding.

Now, let's talk about that ripple effect. Your transformation doesn't just impact you; it sends waves through your family, friends, and even acquaintances. When you embrace change and pursue growth, you inspire those around you to do the same. It's like a domino effect. One person's courage can spark a movement, encouraging others to break free from their own limitations.

Think of someone you admire. Maybe they shared their struggles, their victories, or even their failures. Did that inspire you? I bet it did! That's the beauty of vulnerability. When you're honest about your journey, you give others permission to be real, too. You create a safe space for them to explore their own paths, and that's powerful.

Building a community around these shared experiences is vital. It's not just about you anymore; it's about all of us. By connecting with others, you create a support system that lifts everyone up. You share resources, advice, and encouragement. You celebrate each other's wins, no matter how small. And when someone stumbles, you're there to help them back up.

Let's break it down a bit. Here are some practical steps you can take to inspire others through your journey:

1. **Be Authentic**: Share your true self. Talk about your struggles, your fears, and your victories. The more real you are, the more others will connect with you.

2. **Use Storytelling**: Weave your experiences into stories. People remember stories far better than they remember facts. Paint a picture with your words. Let them see, feel, and experience your journey.

3. **Encourage Others to Share**: Create spaces—whether online or in-person—where people feel safe to share their stories. This could be a blog, a social media group, or a local meetup. Encourage open dialogue and support.

4. **Celebrate Progress**: Acknowledge the small wins, both in your journey and in others'. Celebrate those moments. They're the steppingstones to greater achievements.

5. **Be a Mentor**: Offer your guidance to those who are just starting out. Share what you've learned, but remember, it's not about dictating the path; it's about guiding them as they find their own way.

6. **Stay Connected**: Keep the conversation going. Check in on others, offer support, and continue to share your journey. This builds a lasting community.

7. **Lead by Example**: Your actions speak volumes. Show others what it means to live authentically and pursue growth. Be the change you want to see.

Remember, the goal here isn't to be a superhero or to have all the answers. It's about being human sharing your journey, embracing vulnerability, and lifting each other up.

Your story matters. It's a thread in the fabric of our collective experience. So, don't shy away from sharing it. The world needs your voice. It needs your light. You never know who might be waiting for your words to inspire them to take that first step toward their own transformation.

As you move forward, keep this in mind: every time you share your story, you plant seeds of hope and inspiration in others. Those seeds can grow into something beautiful—a community of individuals striving for growth, change, and connection.

So, get out there and start sharing. Your journey is a beacon for those who are lost in the dark. Shine bright, my friend. The world is waiting for your light.

Chapter 15

Envisioning Your Future

Creating a vision for your future is like planting a seed in the fertile soil of your dreams. You've got to nurture it, water it, and give it sunlight. And that's where a vision board comes in. It's not just a collection of pretty pictures and quotes; it's a tangible representation of your aspirations, a vibrant collage that whispers, "Hey, you can do this!" every time you walk by it.

Picture this: you're sitting in your favorite chair, a warm cup of coffee in hand, and you glance over at that vision board. There's that image of the cozy cabin in the woods you've always dreamed of the words "Fearless" and "Adventurous" splashed across the top, and a reminder of the book you want to write nestled in there too. It's all there, laid out in front of you, a visual feast of your goals and desires. Each image, each word, is a beacon guiding you toward your future.

Now, let's talk about visualization. It's a powerful tool that goes hand-in-hand with your vision board. You might be wondering, "How does just imagining my goals help me achieve them?" Well, think of it like this: when you visualize your success, you're essentially rehearsing for the big performance. Your brain doesn't know the difference between a real experience, and one vividly imagined. So, when you picture yourself achieving your goals, you're wiring your mind for success. You're building confidence, clarity, and a roadmap to follow.

Take a moment to close your eyes and imagine your future. What do you see? Maybe it's you standing on stage, sharing your story with a room full of inspired faces. Or perhaps it's you launching that business you've always wanted. Whatever it is, hold onto that image. Let it fuel your fire. Visualization is like a compass, pointing you in the right direction, reminding you of what you're working toward.

But here's the thing: achieving those dreams requires more than just dreaming. It demands commitment—commitment to lifelong learning and growth. Life is a constant evolution, and so should you be. The world is changing faster than a cheetah on the hunt, and if you want to keep up, you've got to be willing to learn and adapt.

Think of yourself as a sponge, soaking up knowledge and experiences. Read books, take courses, attend workshops—whatever it takes to expand your horizons. Every new piece of information you gather is like a building block for your future. You're constructing a solid foundation that will support your dreams and aspirations.

And let's not forget the importance of reflection in this process. Take time to pause and assess your journey. What have you learned? What challenges have you overcome? Each experience, whether good or bad, is a lesson in disguise. Embrace it.

Now, I know what you might be thinking: "But what if I fail?" Well, let me tell you something—failure is just a steppingstone on the path to success. It's not the end; it's a part of the journey. Each stumble, each misstep, is an opportunity to learn and grow.

So, as you create your vision board and practice visualization, keep this in mind: you're not just aiming for a destination; you're enjoying the ride. Embrace the process of learning and evolving. Celebrate your small wins along the way. Each little victory is a reminder that you're moving forward, inch by inch, step by step.

To make this more actionable, let's break it down into some simple steps.

1. **Create Your Vision Board**: Gather images, quotes, and anything that resonates with your goals. Arrange them in a way that inspires you. Hang it somewhere you'll see it every day.

2. **Practice Visualization**: Set aside a few minutes each day to close your eyes and imagine your future. Feel the emotions associated with achieving your goals. Let that energy propel you forward.

3. **Commit to Lifelong Learning**: Identify areas where you want to grow. Sign up for a class, read books, or find a mentor. Embrace every opportunity to expand your knowledge.

4. **Reflect Regularly**: Take time to assess your progress. What have you learned? What can you improve? Reflection is key to growth.

5. **Embrace Failure**: Shift your mindset. View failure as a lesson, not a setback. Each experience is a chance to learn and grow stronger.

6. **Celebrate Small Wins**: Acknowledge your progress, no matter how small. Each step forward is a victory worth celebrating.

Remember, my friend, the journey to your future is just as important as the destination. So, as you envision your future, know that you have the power to shape it. You're not just a dreamer; you're a doer. And with each step you take, you're getting closer to the life you've always imagined.

So, go ahead—create that vision board, visualize your success, and commit to learning. The world is waiting for you to shine. You've got this!

Printed in Great Britain
by Amazon